POEMAS ANTE EL CATAFALCO: GRIEF AND RENEWAL

To Carmen
With love and affection
and admiration —

Always your friend,

[signature]

Albuquerque NM
October 8, 2014

POEMAS ANTE EL CATAFALCO: GRIEF AND RENEWAL

By examining death from a wide range of angles, Donna Snyder opens the door to a first-rate vision of resurrection: one rooted beyond the humanness of oblivion and permanent sleep and into the greenness of life and wide-open skies. Without question, *Poemas ante el Catalfaco: Grief and Renewal* is a portrait of an artist who has succeeded in turning tragedy into grace and death into a fine portrait of life's renewing energy.

> **Lawrence Welsh's** eighth book, *Begging for Vultures: New and Selected Poems, 1994-2009*, won the New Mexico-Arizona Book Award and other recognitions. His work has appeared in over two hundred publications.

Donna Snyder's poems stand "ante el catafalco," before the casket of each of the loved whose passages are the twining thread that runs through this book. With a driven, bilingual energy sometimes solemn, sometimes furiosa, she addresses loss so great it can only be taken standing up. "The dead reach out across the desert / burned like bricks by the enemy sun / beyond the corpses / a litter of bottles emptied of life / make a trail to the border with its gaudy signs." In this border country the poet laments the passages of men: her father, a husband, a lover, and in some way, Christ himself, as their male energy moves through her life, through her yard, through her house, through her desert country, to the border.

> **Lee Ballentine**, poet and surrealist, is the author of seven books of poems and editor of the anthology *POLY*. He has published in every decade since the 1960s.

Death is the universal intimate stranger, replacing loved ones with a void. The void cannot be filled but art can rise from agony. Donna writes through her losses, cloaks herself in memories against the darkest nights until eventually she sees the moon brighten up the sky.

> **Belinda Subraman**, desert Southwest poet, writer, blogger, podcaster and video artist, is the author of *Blue Rooms, Black Holes, White Lights* from Unlikely Books.

Reading *Poemas ante el Catafalco: Grief and Renewal* is a multi-dimensional healing experience. These visceral poems are the hum of one clean arrow slung straight from the center of beingness, from Donna's heart, but also the universal heart. Her poems bleed in the way that life makes us all bleed, and ground the reader in a deeply embodied, passionate reality. Yet they are as magical as they are real, cocooning the reader in luminous mythic threads.

> **Cathleen Daly** is a poet and writer of children's books. Her book, *Prudence Wants A Pet*, was nominated for the Monarch and Golden Sower Awards, and was an ALA Notable Children's Book for 2012.

Grief is a mirror-cast of what the world inflicted on the writer. So writing about grief is not about what the world is, not its sadness, not its joy, but about the shadows of those emotions. Reading *Poemas ante el Catafalco: Grief and Renewal* is essentially decoding those events, retrieving them from Snyder's vivid abstracts. Her grief makes her house the gibbet for herself. She announces, "I am alone. No one I know is in this shell of brick and wood." These poems lay the path to recovery with fired tiles.

> **Kushal Poddar**, a native of Kolkata, India, writes poetry, scripts and prose and is published worldwide. He is the author of *A Place For Your Ghost Animals*. His poem, "All Our Fictional Dreams," is published in several anthologies in the Indian continent and in America. His forthcoming book is *Kafka Dreamed Of Paprika*.

In her book *Poemas ante el Catafalco: Grief and Renewal* Donna Snyder creates an atmosphere. Regardless of intent or muse, the words take second stage to the emotion of the story of her journey. This is a must have.

> **Christian Lawrence Alvarez** is the author of *The Beat* and 11 other collections of poetry.

Donna Snyder takes us on a journey as she comes to peace with grief for the men she has lost, recreating both the ethos of creative and passionate lives cut short and how she has been left to cope. Her poems on renewal present the continuance of life in a world that often forgets and is not easily ready to forgive. Snyder weaves nature and the environment into her work and as these elements are brought to life they embody characters in her journey.

> **Miguel Juárez**, MLS, MA, is the author of *Colors on Desert Walls: the Murals of El Paso*, and is a doctoral student at the University of Texas at El Paso.

Donna Snyder's hauntingly lovely book is filled with poems which tell the story of loss, grief, and renewal. In their aggregate, the poems follow an arc which moves the reader from the experience of keen personal grief and loss to a more communal sense of bereavement. Ultimately we are buoyed by the resilient spirit of the speaker of these poems as she moves from the personal to the public.

> **Marguerite Maria Rivas**, M.A., D.Litt. is a professor at the City University of New York.

DESIGN EDITOR
NICK ADAM RODRIGUEZ

COVER ARTIST
VICTOR HERNÁNDEZ
Angel in Decline
(oil on bedsheet)

Poemas ante el Catafalco: Grief and Renewal

Donna J. Snyder

Printed In The United States Of America
First Edition 2014

ISBN: 978-0-9850342-2-1

Chimbarazu Press
70 Prospect Pk. SW
Brooklyn New York 11215
United States

http://chimbarazupress.com

Chimbarazu Press

In memory of my beloved muertitos

Roy K. Snyder (November 29, 1921 - March 9, 2005)
Daddy, your baby loves and misses you always.

Jesús Guzmán (May 27, 1955 - April 16, 2001)
Compañero, your love will sustain me para siempre.

Mario Colín (July 9, 1959 - October 5, 2013)
My husband, our love and your legacy shall not be diminished.

Raquel Nájera Duran (April 23, 1928 - December 29, 2009)
Señora, you are the goddess of the Tumblewords Project and forever
in my heart.

CONTENTS

FOREWORD

The poems in *Poemas ante el Catafalco* by Donna Snyder are the cries of a heart's distress, unadulterated grief laid bare not for revelation but for the ponder heart's reflection. If confession is good for the soul, then reflection is good for the grief of loss. There may be no greater grief than the grief of loss. But that grief is vitiated by *leger de langue* and its lexicon of memory.

A catafalco is a raised bier used to support a casket, coffin, or body of a deceased during a funeral or memorial service. A catafalco may be used to stand in place of the body at the absolution of the dead or used during masses of the dead.

In "The day the artist died," Snyder writes:

> A black dove nests in the arms of my Bird of Paradise.
> He leaves me feathers,
> in memory of the one who's gone.

In "Feather of Death" she elaborates on that theme. It is this elaboration so skillfully woven that threads the architecture of *Poemas ante el Catafalco*. This is a gifted work by a gifted poet.

Memory is like rolling tumbleweeds herded by the vagaries of the wind wither no particular destination save that obstructed by wire, to lay fallow-deep in recollection shared with the wind. The poem is indeed a testament to the sacrament of memory. It is that sacrament that allays Snyder's poetry from the maudlin, giving it rise to prayer, appropriate *ante el catafalco*.

The anguish of the poetry is captured by the expression "Catastrophe is our only home," in the poem "A neon desert the only sea." But it is not only catastrophe the poet sees in the loss of the beloved and those loved, as memory weaves a skein of images that offer a glimmer of light in the murmurs of the heart.

There's a song in Spanish that asks: "Porque te fuiste?" Why did you go? It is the same question that Margaret asks in Wordsworth's "The Ruined Cottage" as she waits for her husband's return from the sea, day after day until the end of her life.

There are no answers that grief can provide—"shadows merge with dark space" and "a dying heart" cries out "for a soothing hand" as "silent frogs fiddle and drum." The grief heralds that "dark times have come." Who will comfort the bereaved through the long night when the snow lies deep upon the ground? The balm of memory will be her comfort.

Though these are poems of grief, there is "a green door" of portent in their scaffolding. And renewal awaits in "oatmeal and cinnamon tea." A master poet has crafted this collection.

Felipe de Ortego y Gasca, Ph.D., *taught the historic first course on Chicano Literature, is the principal scholar for this literary movement, and created the taxonomy for its study. Dr. Ortego founded the first Chicano Studies Program in Texas, among many other ground-breaking achievements. He has written and published poetry, essays, memoirs, plays, critiques, songs, scholarly articles and text books for over sixty years.*

Preface

My publisher, Guillermo (Wil) Echanique Winn, approached me with the concept for this book shortly after my husband, artist Mario Colín, died unexpectedly at age 54. At the time, I was too paralyzed by mourning to do more than continue the writing which was a natural outgrowth of my emotional state. Mario's death also triggered renewed grief over the deaths of my father Roy K. Snyder, my buen compañero Jesús Guzmán, who fell to his death at age 44 fourteen years previously, and my dear friend Raquel Duran. These deaths also lead to a struggle with aging and my own inevitable demise.

A few months after Wil spoke to me, I was able to look at both the new poems and older poetry written at the time of the death of my other loved ones. I also discovered pieces written in response to public tragedies and catastrophes. These events often triggered in me anger and despair, and I would sort through those feelings while writing and reading aloud at weekly workshops presented by the Tumblewords Project, a grassroots literary project which I founded in 1995 and continue to coordinate to this day.

My reaction to less personal tragedy originates both in my native sensibility and in my work as a social justice advocate in Texas and New Mexico. As an attorney, I chose to represent indigenous people, immigrant workers, and people with disabilities. This work, occupying over three decades of my life, honed my understanding of the difficulties and even horrors life can present. As well, the experience deeply influenced my poetry.

My poetry is also influenced by the physical environment where I live, the mountainous Chihuahua Desert, and especially by la cultura fronteriza, the culture of the Borderlands where we speak Spanglish, a mix of Mexican border Spanish and West Texas English. Fronterizos/as use calo, a special slang, and non-standard Spanish, and are idiosyncratic in their use of accent marks, with some people adamant about the use of accents in the spelling of their own names and others equally determined that no accents be used—practices which would be considered incorrect in other regions where Spanish is spoken and written. Spanglish IS el idioma fronterizo—what I speak at work, at home, and in public during all of my daily encounters. It is the language used in much of my poetry. To underscore the daily use of this language, I follow the lead of many scholars and activists who do not italicize words in either Spanish or English, letting both languages stand as equal.

Wil's suggested structure, to include both poems written from the immediate aftermath of loss and those written as part of the healing process, proved helpful, rescuing me from spiraling more deeply into sorrow. I found poetry written around the time of my marriage to Mario, which had naturally aided my recovery from the earlier loss of Jesús. I also discovered poems written in particularly happy or fruitful periods, which served to move me forward from desolation to renewed pleasure in life's joys.

Thank you for sharing my account of these experiences. I hope you find this book of benefit as you encounter the inevitable losses and sorrows that come to us all.

Donna J. Snyder
El Paso, Texas

ACKNOWLEDGEMENTS

I received help regarding format and copy editing from poets **Robin Scofield** and **Carly Bryson** and legal secretary **Josefina Jauregui**. The artist **Victor Hernández**, who provided the cover's compelling visual image, *Angel in Decline*, also assisted in tasks involved in the assembly of the manuscript and provided the author's photograph. **Nick Adam Rodriguez** provided outstanding work as the layout artist, along with copy editing, and general wizardry. These friends and colleagues will have my lifelong gratitude for their support and guidance.

Guillermo (Wil) Echanique Winn, my publisher, envisioned this book, and provided encouragement and support in myriad ways throughout the process. His confidence in me made it possible for me to persevere. He also reminded me almost daily that "Life is beautiful." These are gifts that can never be repaid, except with my endless affection and respect.

I want to express particular thanks to my mother, **Mary Lou Williams Snyder**, and my two sisters, **Cheryl** and **Diane Snyder**, who together with my father, **Roy**, provided the foundation for my love of books.

PART ONE

GRIEF

Death arrives among all that sound
like a shoe with no foot in it, like a suit with no man in it,
comes and knocks, using a ring with no stone in it, with no
finger in it,
comes and shouts with no mouth, with no tongue, with no throat.
Nevertheless its steps can be heard
and its clothing makes a hushed sound, like a tree.

Pablo Neruda, "Nothing But Death"

BEREAVEMENT

The smell of barbershops makes me break into hoarse sobs.
The only thing I want is to lie still like stones or wool.

Pablo Neruda, "Walking Around"

No one I know here with me

In the dark all the pages look blank, shadow against shadow.
Scarlet lightning fractures the black of my eyelids.
A cephalopod wraps itself around my sternum in fury.
Screams silent in the alienated night recede unheard,
tears stifled in the tactile geometry of textiles.

Everything is the same color without light.
Black is not the absence of color, but the presence of all.

No one takes the frightened hand from about the throat.
No one calms remembered fear in the strangled neck.
No one's heavy breath reassures from that other space.
I am alone. No one I know is in this shell of brick and wood.
No one I know remains here beside me.

Despair makes for strange bed fellows.
Lie down with dogs, rise up with fleas.

The cruelest month

in memory of Jesús Guzmán

April winds rage in with a renegade posse of dust,
weather's bad boys intent on stealing a body's air.
And one cruel April, Jesús was killed on Easter Monday.
Day after resurrection Sunday, he fell from Jacob's Ladder.
It was the sudden stop that killed him.

Undoubtedly ¡Ay cabrón! frozen on his lips when he hit the ground,
a tiny blood red rose quivering alone in the wind-blasted dirt.
Jesús killed, an angel fallen from the heavens.
Declared dead on the scene, mad scientists shocked him
until his heart resumed its beat, like all fallen angels
determined to return to lost paradise.
Declared dead at the scene on Easter Monday.
Declared dead in ICU on Tuesday afternoon.
Then on the third day they took away his tubes and wires,
and his heart beat for another hour.

He fought Miss Death until they declared him dead
all over again.
No resurrection,
except in the memories of children he taught to be poets,
or the minds of workers who crossed the borders
from there to here.
He crossed over from this life to the next one,
neither from here nor from over there.
And the mesas crashed onto the freeway like waves.
The spring night bled teardrops like falling stars
because he's still cheated of air.
Cheated of words.

Cheated of life.
The world cheated of him and his corazón, too soon.
Jesús was killed on Easter Monday and Tuesday and Wednesday.
His heart tan fuerte it took three times to kill him.

His death scene punctuated by the street's beat
and the lullabies of the bereft.
Now the world is so cold and lonely in April,
when the winds carry the spirits of dead vatos to remind us
just how cruel a month can really be.

Lamentation

I am the stigmata in Jesus's hands & feet,
purple flesh a cup for putrefaction.
I am the green odor emanating from his god's wounds.
Jesus has delivered his painful flesh and ravished spirit
into the faithful arms of Morfeo.
Sleep is his only friend,
oblivion his only love.

I am the despair that compels his hand
to mutilate his own flesh.
I am the mutilated flesh.
I am the sad blood singing him to sleep.
I am the sad blood.
I am the blood on Jesus's hands.
I am the lonely earth
beneath his ravaged feet.

To Titian's Ariadne

My body twists and turns in naked sorrow,
my love gone on his strange and lonesome journey,
without me.

I am left exposed, undraped,
grasping scarves around my fleshiness,
silken shields red and blue.

Vulnerable to passion and dissolution.
Exposed alike to beasts and the naked sky.
My red hair is a noose about my neck.

I am eager for the grave.
The senses compel me
to lose my abandoned flesh to pleasure.

Oblivion lurks on cat feet in the wild dark.

The day the artist died

in memory of Mario Colin

Today the artist died.
Drummers drum the dancers' steps,
firm and heavy beneath the trees.
The dancers dance a prayer.
A black dove leaves a feather at my back door,
another on my front step.
The sky paints itself a heaven.

The Queen of Heaven
fades and crumbles on adobe walls,
her flesh cracked and weathered
by the unrelenting sun.
Without the artist to create her,
without his hands,
stained blue and gold,
how will She know herself in all her glory?

How will She love herself
without his devotion? Each stroke of his brush
another prayer. Each star placed deliberately
on her cloak by his knowing touch.
Her double chin an invocation.
Her sorrowful eyes, a lament.
Each precise shade he adds, a request,
"Pray for us sinners,
now and at the hour of our death."

How will She know to pray
without the clasped hands of the artist
devoted to Her glory?

Who will paint the Queen of Heaven?

Who will kiss the stained hand of her most devoted son?

In the park the drums have ceased to call us to the dance.
The dancers have packed their rattles and hoops
and gone away.
A black dove nests in the arms of my Bird of Paradise.
He leaves me feathers,
in memory of the one who's gone.

The master's dog

Some days the red dog does not wag his tail. His water feels like soup even in the shade. The pigeons steal his chow and the mockingbird annoys him with its car alarm mimesis. Some yards have no grass. Some yards are covered with stones called red dog gravel and stickers strong enough to bite through the thickest callous. Some days even the shadow is not enough.

My two Diegos

There on the shelf beneath the blue glass bottles,
an altar to Santa Frida la dolorisima,
one of my special saints. She has left her mark on me,
imbued me with a certain mexicanidad.
She was rebel and rabble rouser, contraventional,
the surrealist in my woodshed.
Her blood runs in my veins,
her corazón visible and pierced
como San Sebastian, un venado espinado.
Her spirit is in me.

I married Diego twice, as she did,
even though I never divorced him.
My first querido sapo fell from heaven to his death,
the only thing left of him on the scene a miniature rose.
The stain of his cranial fluid mixed with blood came out his nose.
The world became a noisy, hostile place.
No one to protect me.
Bandits demanded my money
because they thought they deserved it more than I did.

Abraham Lincoln martyred on Avenida de Beníto Juárez,
just one more dead president for the masses.
All my masks broken on the floor.
All the broken pottery and splintered wood.
The fallen angel tumbling over a red devil with blue eyes.
The Huichol jaguar pawned for fools gold.
My own demons replaced with another's.

My second Diego, el panzón with paint under his nails,
stood with me at the bench before an old man in a black robe.
We took the oath of office,

put flowers on the altar of Santa Frida,
tattooed la Virgencita on the back of a devotee
because every promise necessitates a blood sacrifice.
Gold leaf flying everywhere like Frida's saffron.
Diego's pistol falling from his pants while no one looked.

I wait for a sign from Santa Frida to tell me when it's over.
She just holds me in her lap, our sagrados corazones
connected by the umbilicus mundi,
all the Diegos asleep as if dead.
All the Diegos dead,
chrysanthemums sprouting from my head.

Feather of death

in memory of Roy K. Snyder

I. Remembered strength

Out of the turquoise foam a magician rises
wheels around
His cloak blossoms around his shoulders
Feather of death

It's one more time around the bitter wheel
Dust shimmers with remembered strength
A dying lion shudders
clambers over doomed swans
thrusts a naked head into memory's wildest moments
Crimson berries gather in the house of the heart
Four chambers shut one after another
Strength remembered

Tree limbs shake against a bleached sky
like death
Not doom
Just death

II. Grief

My mouth won't form words
I'm not sure about pearly gates
or if there is a better place awaiting
somewhere in some sweet bye & bye
All I see is white blue sky that hurts my eyes
rutted earth packed hard and unforgiving

chamisa too dry to give up its sweet smell
Empty river a bed unmade and hard to lie in
There is a face the color of ash
carved by the elemental forces
White hair on the head of the old one

A silver lion dying
One more time around the bitter wheel

A man stays young so long
as someone needs no excuse to show affection
A woman stays young as long as she moves her body with joy
A fool sees beauty only in the dewy young
believes only the young & firm give pleasure to the senses
thinks only youth deserves the ecstasies
found in a life fully lived

Look at this world
It's old as dirt
Yet even when it craves a humid embrace
its ancient beauty is dazzling as the sight of angels
in all their angel glory
bent down to stroke thirsting flesh with an incandescent kiss

III. Wheel within the wheel

My mind ceases to make thought
at that place where public life shoves itself
into what should be secret
I fall deep into a panic that stems
from a sense of being vulnerable to the pack

I tumble into a turquoise lake
Each gasp fills my lungs with murky doom

I open and close my mouth
now a fan of feathers drowned in moonlight
Darkness fractured by light and water

To be alone in the endless abyss
without anticipation of any haven—
the unconscious thought stops the suck of darkness into my lungs
I cease to flail
My feet cold as mountain rain
My eyelids flutter like snow blankets over frozen ponds

My ankles wear bracelets of water-woven grass
My feet touch down on shifting sand and sodden debris
My hands float above my head like naked wings
When they reach the surface they become lace on air

A cloak blossoms around my shoulders
Warm flesh wraps itself around this failing body
Pulls me up and out of milky death
beyond the gloom of sorrow & fear
My pale face breaks the dark waters
Smiles at the moon dancing
bright against the blackest beauty of the windblown sky

Daddy? Are you there?

Daddy has withdrawn
lost to a kaleidoscope world of cable-friendly images
youth & beauty
vigor & wealth
My old sweet Daddy is aloof now
Won't talk to me
Won't give me comfort
His attention off somewhere he can't talk to me about
or won't

Daddy won't read my poems
Doesn't send me email or letters
Can't get my jokes or recall to miss my voice
He's checked out before it's time
bound & determined to get an early start on the road
into the wild blue yonder
without me
Why won't he linger with me yet a little while?
Why not abide yet just a wee bit longer here with me?

Talk to me
Bring me comfort
Abide with me
Daddy? With me?

Gone man gone

in memory of Armando Colín

He's buried in a potters' field
Nothing but tumbleweeds
Stumblebums come to drink and cry
Birds sing that same old cheerless song
My best friend long gone
So gone
Long gone
So gone
So long

A cactus black & broken

dedicated to George Carrizal and all the dead vatos

Like a cactus black & open,
lying among the carrizo,
you have lost your fruit.

Gone with the gypsy river,
muddy and sad,
its flow fouled
by the detritus of broken lives.

I see your form as it once was,
vital and full of ardor,
now pierced & broken,
seedless and without juice.

Your flesh blackened
with torment.
Your loves rusted
with futility & sorrow.

I hear the grieving wind,
scarlet in the reeds,
calling your name.

DESPAIR

and they don't know
why harsh winds whistle in my poems,
the narrow uneasiness of a coffin,
winds untangled from the Sphinx
who holds the desert for routine questioning

César Vallejo, "Have You Anything To Say In Your Defense?"

Cantata of the Red Rock Shadow

1.
The halo around incandescence
whites out my eyes.
Background sounds lull into dull
white noise.

Images fragment, sounds of trains
dopple through planes,
the geometric barriers of architecture.
Negative space the only true space.
The page bears fruit.
Outside the mesquite thrashes the air,
unhappy again that it is spring here.
In spring the wind gods vanquish all life,
succulence gone to wind and dust,
a cantata created from fragmentation,
the apocalyptic present,
the smell of lilac from a neighbor's yard.

A noose dangling like a naked light bulb.
I am thinking nothing not contained
in the halo of a hanging light bulb,
naked in the night.
Nothing.
Always nothing.

2.
Waiting for the knock at the door.
Twin lovers never the twain shall meet.
The beast with two backs broken.
Boys locked in closets of baseball bats.
The fear of rats.
An infant howling for its mother's dugs.

Take this.
Eat.
Bread my body.
Wine my blood.
Easter season brings conflagrations
close to home.
She stumbles beneath the weight of it.
Her cross to bear.
Fire scourges west Texas.
What phoenix can we pray to rise up?
Low in the grave he lay.
Our savior.
Waiting the coming day.
Our lord.
Her cross to bear.
Her life to lose.
Her grasp on life, loose.
Breath turned brown.
Death's earthy ground.

3.
Sound of water running.
Telephone ringing.
Rock of ages cleft for me singing.
He is dead and we are left dying.
Sepulchral voices accuse of lying.
The sound of water over rock.
Paper over rock.
Scissors rend paper.
Rock breaks scissors.
Superfluous options.
A liar's waiver, voice haunting.
Spirits evaporate to dust.
Trains thunder through the barrio.
The sound of motion.
Steel on steel.

Hurry before the spirits steal
what's left of sanity.
Peal after clamorous peal.
Bells ring warnings.
Effulgence pouring.
Someone's at the door—
out the door go running.

4.

The murmur of women praying.
Drunken lilies
nod their heads like sages.
Irish poets sing in French.
Smell the scent of angels falling.
Bells clamor above death's stench.
Sparrows huddle, not the least of these.
Desertscape dessicated and austere.
Heaven the sound of water running
over rocks somewhere hidden.
Somewhere out there a choir of angels.
beat boys with baseball bats.
Adesti fidelis.

5.

Four flaming drays running away.
Everywhere the smell of excrement
and fire.
The life as sacrament.
The poem as testament.

The Sunday news

1.

From the Associated Press:

Dolphins found shot, slashed, stabbed, and missing jaws.
Mutilations and other injuries recorded in recent months.
One found dead near Gaultier had a hole made by a 9 mm bullet.
Scientists who study marine mammals report four recent strandings
and on a recent Friday, another dolphin dead on Deer Island,
a piece of his jaw removed.

This just in:

Nietzsche was right about God,
and I am left alone in an incomprehensible world.
Sentient creatures who might have the answer I seek
die bleeding peace into a dirtied ocean,
its waters fouled with despair that cannot be scrubbed clean.

Dateline Damascus:

Children and journalists mutilated and killed by bombs,
blown into the meaningless abyss of a zero sum game.
They failed to learn the rules of play.

In other news:

People shot, slashed, stabbed—
an endless litany of horror born of greed for capital or power.

Next up, commentary:

Nothingness lurks behind images and words.

2.

The tears of God fall brittle upon the fat of my cheeks
as from a frozen deity,
stripped of omniscience,
denuded of omnipotence,
omnipresent no more.
An arrowless quiver, the body unflung at its mark,
and I wait for the somethingness
born of the limbs of the mother of all gods.
She whose breast will protect me.
She who will take me into her brown arms and cover me
with a blanket of green
floating in a nearly endless blue,
spinning through the infinite dark.

A neon desert the only sea

1.
Awareness moves to the right
Electric asters line a green sky
Brake lights baffle the eyes
(Are you paying attention?)
Traffic moves to the right

Think of Louisiana—
Think of Japan—
People disappeared
Structures on stilts still
can't out walk the waves
Fissured world shifts in its sleep
as sure as the earth beneath your feet

This may be the only world we know
Secrets and lies in camouflage
The stranger's smile all teeth and eyes
Detainees in your back yard
herded like cattle into the corralón
Downtown old men still hide
numbers tattooed on wrists
or nopales inked on foreheads

Catastrophe is our only home now
Dying cougars shot more dead
Unknown bodies beneath the ground
Spying soldiers spread across the sky
A neon desert the only sea
Even metals gone to driest dust
Hear the sound of air through shell

Scent of water glosses the lips of statues
Birds in tree tops sing departure
(There's about to be an accident)
Our Mama on the wall wears green and blue
She stands on the moon
Blots out the sun

2.
Birds gather in tree tops praying
for all the people dead and gone
Dancers dance with feathers and shells
Mama's starry cloak shelters her Son
with the nopal tattooed on his forehead

Pray for mercy
Pray for the woman who lives in a car
The detainees in our own back yard
Men with guns at every gate
People disappeared on the river edge
deprived of the solace of rivers and rocks
Our Mama damp with migrant workers' sweat

Lights wander the other edge of darkness
Nothing sure but this earth beneath our feet
(Are you paying attention?)
Secrets and lies with teeth and eyes
This is your home now
Another day another catastrophe
It's the only world we've ever known
Earthworks break into thunder claps
Random red lights baffle the eyes

Birds falling from the dying blue
Lost fish floating in the dying sea

Dead hands

The dead reach out across the desert,
burned like bricks by the enemy sun.

Beyond the corpses,
a litter of bottles emptied of life
makes a trail to the border with its gaudy signs.

Down the highway,
a panel truck hides its contraband behind a locked door.
Inside the odor of bodies warns the night sky
to open its arms to death's bounty.

The desert stretches,
a merciless sea of boiled blood waiting for the coming sun.

Only the desperate
believe the lies of the coyote.
(Coyote tricked the Holy Ones out of their fire
and gave it to the People along with this scorched earth.)

Somewhere the names of workers are written
like beads between fingers.

Somewhere fields still and quiet
wait for dead hands to harvest poisoned fruit.

A wave of a thousand bodies

Earth quake in Japan
(registered in Texas)
Gargantuan waves
Bodies and buildings swept to sea
On shore nuclear melt down
Fuel rods stripped and dry
No water but the excess sea
Japan assures its people and the world
everything is "contained"
Go, go Godzilla

A wave of one thousand bodies
On shore nothing but debris
The smell of Death
Officials report no more body bags
Overcapacity crematoria
No shelter
No water
No food

A wave of a thousand bodies
The land of a thousand cranes
The sins of someone else's fathers
visited upon children born of the H bomb
Martial law
Travel restrictions
Entire towns obliterated
Nothing left but rubble
The smell of Death everywhere

And on the other side of the world
zealots speak of divine retribution
Denounce godless materialists and atheists

Pray to an angry father whose impenetrable greatness
is not at all complex to the true believers
a greatness that calls for scourge and animosity
and the smell of Death everywhere

Radioactivity spans the world in days
hits the Pacific coast of North America
The U.S.A. assures its people "No cause for alarm"
"Just a little soap and water
and all better" (says the U.S. Navy)

A precipitous drop in the Nikkei due to the calamities
Japan's banks vow to flood money markets with yen
The projected costs of repairs are in the trillions
The temples of the gods of Hydrogen unappeased
Wall Street is insecure
Just how many more deaths can the market bear?

The per share cost of power
measured in terms of Hello, Kitty backpacks
abandoned by little girls lost to the sea

TRAGEDY

At night I listen to their phantoms
shouting in my ear
shaking me out of lethargy
issuing me commands . . .
to break up our sleep
to come awake
to shake off once and for all
this lassitude.

Claribel Alegría, "Nocturnal Visits"

Book of Ezckicl 16-20

1. The prophecy

Every time I think of Zeke
my throat grows together in angry fear.
My mind fills with electronica,
snatches of incomprehensible speech,
the sound of lock and load,
the terror of the state upon us.

Wooden handles rape our dark places.
Video training films teach torture.
Shouting workers are treated like words are bombs.
We can't hear ourselves if thoughts turn to shame.
Goatherds murdered by stupid kids in camouflage
carrying guns.

Fear at the bridge coming back from the other side.
Black boots. Black pants. Black shirts. Black dogs.
Border reality a constitution-free zone,
assertions of authority to fuck with you ubiquitous.
The best arsenal a funny uncle's money can buy.
The militarization of the border rampant and real.

But Zeke lived in Redford near the Rio Grande.
He lived there in a village in desert pastureland,
an American goatherd born and bred.
Living here in Texas on the border of us and them,
Zeke took his family's flocks to pasture each day.
No one knew soldiers were there.

A boy killed by soldiers he didn't even know existed.
The radio's static and spinning truth confuses grief.

Marines in the arroyos take aim at shepherd boys.
U.S. soldiers killing U.S. civilians.
My throat closes in anaphylactic horror.
Incomprehensible speech all over the news.
My brain jams like a radio receiver in time of war.
The terror of the state is upon us and we are silent.
My thoughts turn to an ancient prophecy of our shame—
the sons and daughters sacrificed,
children slaughtered only to be devoured,
an offering made by fire like the seer warned.

Soldiers killing innocents, a sacrifice by fire
for fear a shepherd's stone might yet fell the beast.

2. Esekiel Hernández, Jr. (May 14, 1979 - May 20, 1997)

In Redford they called him Zeke. He lived there all his life as did his parents, and was a good boy according to the village priest. He belonged to the Future Farmers of America, a simple boy, 18 and not yet out of high school, but a willing student said his teachers. In the Hernández family he had the job that often goes to younger children. He herded goats. He took his goats to pasture, spent the day shooting cans. He never even hit a rabbit, just aimed his World War II era .22 at rusty cans that Redford folks would dump in the arroyos, the way people who live in poor communities without government services often do. A good boy Zeke was, quiet with a ready smile.

The marine who shot Zeke dead waited with his friends more than twenty minutes before reporting the killing, the "incident" as the military would describe it. Those boys sat there in their camouflage, chewing gum and making plans, and did not call for medical assistance. Neither did they render aid themselves. They justified the killing saying the 18 year old goatherd presented a threat by throwing stones and shooting his old .22. The town of Redford went silent with shock at the news. No one knew Marines were on secret patrol in their area. In this town of simple pleasures and quiet pastimes, no one knew Marines were taking aim at the innocence of shepherd boys.

Jasper, Texas June 9, 1998

in memory of James Byrd, Jr.

I am the handsome uncle and the so-called "nigger"
flesh fallen from my bones
I am a martyr
pieces of me strewn two miles along a country road
My daughter is crying
I look at you and you become me and I am become

a cross burning
No man's dick comes to douse the flames
and roses aren't the only thorny creature
within the frame of the world
You make me run the gauntlet of your hate
Before I die a hard-on springs from my head

like Athena from the brow of Zeus
But there are no gods on Mt. Olympus
No one I can implore
No Christ sweating blood
The crucifix is empty

nothing but a cross burning
My daughter ignores the flash of lightning
bows her head before the bitter wine
My people pierce the clouds with a collective howl

Just before I die I long to kiss Medusa
another strong woman scorned
What am I to say before such fear?
My spirit is in pieces
hanging on a chain

Feathers

in memory of Cristóbal Sánchez (April 1982 - July 2003)

Today I write for those who must comfort themselves in times
of distress & sorrow,
for the bruised ones unsheltered from the blows and falls that
brute life bestows,
for she who falls down the stairs and never rises,
breath stolen along with her clarity & will.

Today I write for the ones who fly from the bridge into another
country.
Tierra firma leaps up to welcome the body broken as much by
sadness
as by the implacable embrace of the river bank.
Today I sing Amazing Grace for the sad ones who kiss the earth
then dance their way up a ladder of stars.
Today I chant their names in time with mariachis and feel my
lungs expand.
My poet self seeks to wrest free
words sufficient to turn mortality into everlasting honor.

> *Come to me, cariño.*
> *Let me coax the wordless song from your broken trumpet,*
> *stroke the rhythm from your broken drums,*
> *finger the keys to evanescent pleasure,*
> *trill the crimson of the morning flute.*
> *If I put my lips to the waiting reed*
> *will the broken bones reassemble*
> *and spell your name in feathers across the waiting sky?*

But then I hesitate.
I remember that words are as ephemeral as truth and beauty.
Breath flees.
Ink fades.
Paper crumbles into earth.
Records break like ollas hurled onto the unrelenting floor.
Question marks illuminate the darkness with their finality & droop
but lead me no where.

A crying shame

in memory of Tyler Clementi (December 1991 - September 2010)

I tell you
it is a crying shame.
A mere eighteen year old

Rutgers student,
gifted violinist,
death by drowning.

Jumped off the George Washington Bridge
right into that chilly, nasty Hudson River.

> A boy fearful of ridicule and humiliation.
> A cruel joke made viral by remote control.
> A secret video of boys loving boys.

Two boys—
college boys,
smart and talented,

ready to emerge from the pupa of childhood,
from the extended neotony of modern life.
Maybe it was first love.

A first kiss perhaps,
like electric sugar coursing,

> neural systems awash.
> The soft lips emboldened by the lack of recoil,
> the yielding.

The softness of cheeks.
The nose to the base of the young neck.
The throat.

Those soft humid lips.
That excitement hardening into resolve.
He could be who he was and who he could be.

Any weakness was not in his secret.
Any weakness was sunk low by ignorance.

>That beautiful boy,
>(because all eighteen year olds are beautiful)
>not knowing that outside his circle,

beyond his classmates and family,
a whole world waited, ready to love him,
to love him with a tender ferocity.

Not knowing of this world of women and men
ready to hold him afloat and safe from malice,
to drown him in appreciation and acceptance.

But he thought his future was hopeless
and now it is.

>And now we are left with a video that reveals nothing,
>darkness and shadow,
>no flesh,

the occasional glimmer of unilluminating light.
He was a violinist, I tell you!
A mere college boy,

gifted and smart and ready to flourish
the bow in his practiced hand,
the slender neck held like a flower,

the violin crying and screaming sweetly in his arms,
drowning the very strings in pleasure.

> His hand strong and supple as youth,
> evoking the transcendence of beauty over pain.
> His talent and skill outstripped his worldliness.

And his lungs filled with nasty river water,
his life left behind him on the bridge,
his perceptions distorted by youth and inexperience,

his perceptions wavy grays and blurs as through water.
Just a boy ridiculed and humiliated,
the butt of a joke both reckless and cruel.

The secret video of him and somebody else.
Boys loving boys.

> And now we are left with a video that reveals nothing,
> darkness and shadow,
> no flesh.

No secret scents.
No music.
No beautiful boy.

No boy
ready to embrace the world.
No boy ready to receive the world's embrace.

And I tell you,
it's a crying shame.

Section Four

THE DYING OF THE LIGHT

A hole in my heart has edges
but no lips or tongue

Gene Keller, "Primo Mourns His Amada"

Where a crone sits alone

It's in the cards on the table in front of her nose.
She distracts herself with the taste of milk tea,
illicit lips pursed against the inside of the wrist.
It's all there in the cards for anyone to see.
Stagnation here. Turmoil there.
Permissiveness everywhere at once.
Excessive reliance on the occult arts, perhaps.

She strokes the cards into congruencies.
A Celtoi cross marks the crossroad,
two unparallel lines in a plane.
That leads that away. This leads this away.
They converge here, where a crone sits alone, her head
shrouded in smoke black as a raven feather crown.
The moon is awane and cold.

Shadows merge with dark space.
She pushes and then pulls the cards.
First the five of cups. Then the five of staves.
She whispers, Are you the fifth of anything?
She mutters to no one, Are you the fifth child?
Here is the Tower reversed.
The hermit holds out a lantern.

The moon is hiding its death.
Somewhere tonight the lovers are reversed.
A crown of rose. A chalice of ruby.
Faulty communications. Carelessness and pride.
It's all in the cards, she mutters again.
Dogs fill her lap and quietly sit at her feet,
sweet beasts, asleep, yet ears still awake.

If she moves they take offense. Disappear
into lonely shadow, their absence a black hole
between her legs and belly, taking their puppy
love and memories away with them.
Her hands are moon white,
speckled with evidence of age,
a harsh life lived long and rough.
Someday the moon, she whispers,
will not return with the little Venus.
Someday the moon, she sighs,
will no longer reflect the sun.
Someday the sun will follow
the dogs gone into the dark hole
between the legs of a crooning crone.

Someday the cards will drop and fall.
She sees leaf strewn shoulders of hard roads.
Paths cross each other but lead nowhere.
Somewhere near, the crone sings, tuneless,
in time with the thump and whimper
of a dying heart crying for a soothing hand.

Silent frogs fiddle

There in the mirror behind grimed glass
the face dirtied by blemishes and bruise.
Too small eyes too close together
reflect yellow and red.
The truncated and spotted nose.
Thin lips with edges smudged into freckled skin,
the chin drowned in cheeks and a ruff of flesh

Dim light reflected poorly through passage ways.
There in the mirror that strange face melts
like plastic clocks in the desert sun.
In the shadow above the window masks hang.
Geckos crawl down the nose and up the gate.
A bird mocks the tears in four hundred voices.
Wooden blue eyes and red lips.

A jaguar's growl.
A woman smiles,
peacock feathers fanned across her cheek and brow.
The sounds of horns and barking dogs.
Humid breaths in and out dying flesh.
Somewhere in the rafters a fallen angel.
The sound of snarls punctuated with laughing sobs.

Mimetic mind trails through eye holes and mouth,
somewhere in the back a flaccid string.
Flesh falls into porcelain coffins and painted boxes.
Mirror mists swirl the eye's focus.
Silent frogs fiddle and drum.

The truth of Vikings

The music in her head makes her scared,
as if Vikings still brandished their blades
from the decks of ships fierce as dragons,
afloat in an ageless river.

The leaves are chill flames.
Cold rains obscure the water's source,
hiding it away
like the secret of a woman's aging body.

She is apples and pears.
She ripens in her own sweet skin.
Only the moon can match
the luster of her opalescent belly.

Her mouth makes shadows.
Her fingers are a doorway and her hair a burning bush,
iconic as a religious artifact
still sticky and sweet inside.

She is on route to the end of being
on the back of a red swan.
She is on the way to nothingness made tolerable
by ritual and fire,

and the howling of inconsolate women
who no longer believe
that love will save them from sorrow.
There is no home now (they wail).

There is no safe place.
Death tastes like winter flowers.

She stands so close
she can hear warriors telling each other secrets.

The truth is that neither love nor death
diminishes you.
The way to truth is a life suffered.
The way to truth is a drunken waltz.

She stands so close
her howl is lost in the roar of the music inside her head.
She is wordless before the fact of Vikings,
rain, and a woman's sluggish heat.

Truth is found in a harsh yellow light.

Fierce and fiery to light the long dark

For the dark times I want my lover,
fierce and fiery to light the long night.
He leads me to stone circles,
bonfires on hilltops.
Night birds trill,
sparks arcing in sky lit by a young moon.

Music plays through the trees like light,
secret messages from drunken poets.
The thrill of the longest dark.
Lips against the neck,
beneath the small moon of ear's shadow.
Kisses small and hot as flying embers.

Murmurs in the wintry darkness.
At times the music cries aloud,
wakes the dancers from their starry reveries.
At times the music croons low,
little moans whispered in the dancers' ears,
exhalations in rhythm of December nights.

The dark times have come my love.
Who will hold me through the long night?

PART TWO

RENEWAL

I don't want to go on being a root in the dark,
insecure, stretched out, shivering with sleep,
going on down, into the moist guts of the earth,
taking in and thinking, eating every day.

I don't want so much misery.
I don't want to go on as a root and a tomb,
alone under the ground, a warehouse with corpses,
half frozen, dying of grief.

Pablo Neruda, "Walking Around"

Comfort

The orisha brought me to you in a dream
and I found comfort there.

Your absence a longing within my throat,
  I walk beside the sweet water,
    silent joy etched upon the signpost to freedom.

I have on sturdy shoes and good cotton socks.
I find comfort in the memory of your voice.
I see you along every path.
Your presence comes upon me like balm.

More beautiful with sangria

to Victor Hernández

The artist is rolling papers to make a framework,
something to hide behind
besides the same old drugs and booze and sex.
Nietzsche defined an artist as one who makes something from nothing,
using particular media. (The canvas and paint, the clay and stone.
Look at the hand made from a stump of wood.)
That's why he loved us, said Nietzsche.
That's why the rules don't apply.

We decorate our lives with painted masks,
something scary fashioned to distinguish us from the herd.
Rhythm and words, vibrations harnessed to create structure.
Something to divert the eye from the raw and naked self.
All the urges set free to frolic behind painted masks,
then dance away into the dark.

The trick is to fight the death wish,
take it in your hands and twist it into something new.
The trick is to ride excess into the dirt before it kills you.
The drugs, the sex, the alcohol—
all a flaming structure on which to hang your dying god,
nothing more than paper and string transformed.
Something else to hide behind.

It's all right here in the cards—
ecstasy and passion, a red dress, death in a large hat.
It's just a jump from this existence into something new,
somewhere where the sorry boys burn bright,
a blue October made more beautiful with sangria,
the curve of a dancer's body like the neck of a black swan.

Winter is coming.
The red violin is screaming.
Listen to the secrets of the green gourd—

the marigold path leads to death.
Death parades around in masks to hide its promise.
Quick take a bite of something sweet to hide its bitter kiss.

We got married on Día de los Muertos

for Mario Colín

We got married on Día de los Muertos,
followed the marigold path backwards,
holding hands & running toward ghosts
we'd always tried to flee.
We took them all by surprise.
In our pockets was all the sweet bread we needed,
everything essential to make our journey.

We got married on Day of the Dead.
We clung to each other like tattoos,
calaveras dancing in wedding clothes.
Roses hung across the breast of death.
The smell of dampness dissipated.
Darkness became light.

Who knew we would come together,
find the long lost mates we never knew,
make our pledge?

> *When you fall*
> *I will kneel & put my face on yours.*
> *When I get lost*
> *you promise to come and find me.*

Now I am finding my way slowly to something new,
something scary and fine as the never ending cycle.
And death awakens again to become life,
each year on Día de los Muertos,
the Day of the Dead.

Prepare to ululate

to Nick Adam Rodriguez

Stare the beast in the face, there in the mirror.
Notice the ten-armed monster,
the sleek skin of its fleshy tentacles
wrapped tight
around your throat chakra,
not quite asleep where it has overrun
your heart chakra,
pulsating in the center of your root chakra,
its skin red-black in the refracted light.

Force the air through your throat.
Awaken your voice.
Laugh out loud.
Spell out the meaning—let
the mirth grow into a cackle.
Cast the spell.
Use ALL CAPS for emphasis.

The subtle grace of the crone
at the core of the principle of beauty.
The end cycles into a beginning.
The tentacles ripple into wakefulness.
Feel your throat dilate.
Prepare to ululate.
Feel the giant squid moving in the secret dark.

Let the voice burst through the deep
like exploding stars.

Myth

She falls like a comet through impenetrable dark
Her wail rips through her body & is lost in the abyss
She knows that she is alone and plummeting into Beyond
In her sorrow she strips her clothes,
bangs her fists against her chest

Around her neck hangs a fetish,
a bear long-since flawed by the cleft that flashes through the agate
She looks down toward her belly
The crack in the pendant becomes Shelia Na Gig,
her vulva to the World spread wide above a holy door
She falls through the gap,
tumbles mad into the fissure between her own legs,
her anguished screams swallowed by the endless dark

Come to me my Little Uncle of the Woods
Come to me my Honey Paw
Come to me Unmentionable One
He Who Cannot Be Named heed my call
The stars cease to hurtle through a bereft sky,
fall motionless beyond the lonesome dark

The wounded one holds her in the crook of his arm
Her head finds its place on his shoulder,
her backside's bed his belly so broad
The Owner of the Earth is present
God's Pet
Woman's Balm
He feeds her sweetmeats from his own hand

Einstein smiles

to César Iván

I see Einstein smile and forget his wife.
I spin—
radiant,
ecstatic,
a vortex of energy.
I hear brothers call me dynamo,
the one who moves,
the one who carries water to those who thirst.
I cannot stop the dance within me.
It moves me through the void
beyond selfishness and greed.
Some luminous bond to my sister stars
rescues me from despair.

Brothers smile.
"You can do anything," they say,
"anything you want."
And I am solaced.
And I am reminded—
I am voracious,
indomitable,
a force for good,
a source of bounty.
I am a giant
and Einstein smiles,
beckons me near his mouth.
I feel his breath upon my earlobe.
When he whispers "All time is now,
all energy constant,"

I wonder, is it
that matter does not exist?
Or that it always shall?
The energy of the question goads me with pleasure.
I whirl off, away to find my sister stars.

Mythic sea of *yes*

His smile hangs there like a crescent moon
in a night sky that stretches out forever,
into the liquid abyss of his illicit kiss.

I fling myself out of the chronic despair
where I drown daily, going down
once, twice, and yet again.

I die there, and like a hero punished by fate,
my life returns each day so that, again,
I find myself drowning, going down.

An ardent thirst for passion twists my body
into unfamiliar shapes. But his smile croons
a mythic sea of *yes*,

where no one tells me *never, no more, no.*
He tastes of nutmeg on the tongue.
Buoyed, I surface from the endless night and swim.

A circle of voices keeps rhythm with my strokes—
yes, yes, yes, yes, yes, and yet again, *yes.*
My feet settle firmly on the night-kissed shore.

Eye of god

The words dizzy the blood
make me drunk
entrance me
The uptake of breath
The flush so like desire
The avid search for shared meaning

The flush
The upsurge of pulse
Oxygenated blood races to unneeded organs
moss forgotten on the banks of ephemera
Spring long since gone for good (or ill)

Trunks of trees planted firmly in desert earth
The smell of rain a promise unfulfilled
The bottom of something
The nothing of nothing
What once was now never more to be
Nothing enters nowhere
Nothing entered
Nothing gained
The unspoken lie
The unuttered laughter
The never to be felt again
The never will be the same

Then that rush
that dizzying rush
Words unintended
unanticipated

Eye of god
Around here that's what they call a gushing stream

Dance ferocious magic

Caramel breast let me lick
our secret death
Whisper delicate poet boy
Unravel my naked soul
Dance ferocious magic

over my skin
Eyes dazzled
Warm current
Blue perfume
Essential universe

Skin

I wish for reasons for you to dream about my skin.
The fat pillows it encases.
The frills of stretch marks.
The hirsute patches.
The flaccid cheeks, eyelids, jowls.
The loose, hungry lips.
The hot flesh against your skin chilled
by the naked couch.

You slip beneath my sheets and your cold blood
meets my hot.
Your arms snake beneath my neck,
across my throat,
so close we become twins conjoined by choice.
Your hands warm themselves at my breast.
Your lips and teeth, close against my shoulder.
Your breath against my lonely cheek.
Your skin smooth and hairless as the moon
through my autumn window, so far away.

Minnow slip of the finger

When the artist fell in love
remembering became easier—
the way her face looked before he had ever seen it
The minnow slip of his finger across her speckled wrist
The cinnamon flakes on cream skin
The flush of flesh
Humidity sudden in the desert heat
The monsoon season of the wet country
here in the dry country
This country of drought
where death is nearer than life

The old woman appearing like a large baby
draped in blankets
the color of eggs and wet sand
the soles of her feet
neglected into rust
Look at the desiccating bush
The nopales broad and flat and fat
easily thought dead
flaccid in the hands of a brutal sun
crushed in its grip
Limp crepe

But there amidst all that death
the ruby flash of tuna
waiting for the beard of thorns to be trimmed
Waiting for the teeth
The dripping sweet

The gentling

He nudges her lightly with a knee,
moves her in small ways, communicating
intent without meaning,
mending her sorrows.

Have mercy, she breathes, shudders
as he bites the back of her shoulder,
mouths mysteries
into her hair,

the mane of a horse long mad,
lost in a hostile desert,
coat tattered,
mouth torn and bruised,

bereft of the touch all creatures require.
He gentles her restlessness,
strings stars across her sadness,
strokes her nightmares into a sense of safety.

He fixes the broken fence,
unlocks the gate,
rides her until She rises.
Epona, the horse goddess,
a riot of rebirth racing into her own rain.

Under the fecund moon

Speak to me in Spanish. I'll hear all vowels and no consonants. I'll understand all nouns and no verbs, miss the plot but grasp the emotion. The guttural whispers in my ear like secrets, in my shoulder through teeth clenched, but not in anger.

Speak to me in Spanish. The sound of sweat and heat. Birds drift lazily across the sky on air's pillows, alert to the desert brush for movement, the smell of blood and flesh. A nest built from cactus and rock.

The sunset every shade of carmine. The blood of Christ frosted with snow, smelling of juniper and piñon. The evening sky every flavor of fruit. Sandía. Granada. Sticky sweet magenta of tuna—succulence hidden by thorns. Teeth and claws a must. Juice spilling from whispering lips.

Speak to me in Spanish. The consonants, lost in susurrations, connect directly to the parasympathetic system. Reason left behind in the patch of datura's moon flowers. Angel trumpets' milky blooms under the fecund moon.

I am the sound of the sea

to Xánath Caraza

I am the sound of the shell you hold to your ear, the sound of the ancient sea before this land was desert. I am the sound of the sea behind your eyes shut against the glare of neon shining through your window from the café across the street.

In the night, your breath heavy and your flesh warm, I am the sound of ceramic guitars, once clay, formed with your hands, smoothed and shaped into momentary beauty, behind the dreams in your sleeping eyes. Suspirations and susurrations, secret confessions heard by no one. The simple assent. The unintended exhalation of satisfaction. The chords augmented by calloused hands. The rhythm dictated by you and you alone.

When the morning comes and you sleep still, I trace your cheek bones with my dusty eyes, your breath the desert wind that never ceases. And I am the sound of the sea.

Cinnamon tea

for Jesús Guzmán

Sweet oatmeal and cinnamon tea
wait for me each morning when I wake,
no matter what snarls curled around our throats the night before.

Or maybe agua de melón and toast sit there
next to the napkins from Guatemala,
faded temptations to smile,
to rub my finger across your inner wrist
and sit awhile.

When I get older,
and all I know now gone forever from my grasp,
I will tell the young ones who care to hear,
I knew love and love knew me.
Its name was oatmeal,
toast,
and cinnamon tea.

I clutch my arms about myself and croon

I am a mesa—huge as permanence yet worn down to grit by each storm that hits my flesh. I am an ungentled filly—full of nerve and quick to agitate. I am fire—just when you think it's gone it bursts into a raging flame. I am a retina—I sing my sight to all my nerves. I am a Clydesdale because I am a workhorse for justice.

I am a piece of tissue—people will use me until I disintegrate into nothingness. I am dirty dishes—I always need attention. I am un veterano—disordered by my post-traumatic sensibilities. I am Job—punished and tested beyond comprehension. I am King David because I am blessed by God.

I am a poem because I incite with words and create images in your mind. I am a grocery list—nothing more than a collection of needs. I am like trouble—I never seem to disappear for good. I am like the internet—connected to sentient beings across the world. I am like my clients—I need peace with dignity and grace.

I am like a madman—I wear my troubles about my neck and run naked in the street. I am a cyclone—a force of nature that changes those who find themselves in my path. I am a little Viet Nam—I never back down. I am like film—I collect vicarious trauma and its image appears across my face.

Like an angel falling

1.
My hand hesitates not because my mind is blank,
but rather that it flees each thought from fear,
the fear of consequences, of being too trite
or too self revelatory.

A man asked his motherly wife
why his friend had jumped from the roof like an angel falling.
The bearded lady sighed at just another suicide,
just another person with too many options.

The opposite of commitment is paralysis not freedom.
The issue before us here is the meaning of self-destruction,
yet we only seem to care when the effect
is an unambiguous line between here and not here.

The issue before us is the purpose of choice.
If you're not part of the solution
you will never be able to realize the state of the problem.
The big questions remain unanswered,

like the theory of everything which still explains nothing.
If matter is only denser energy, what is the truth behind $E=Mc^2$?
We must concentrate energy to make something matter,
or just accept that matter really doesn't matter anyhow.

Dark energy is neither the details nor the devil.
All life emerges from a single dark hole.
And like the man who flew from the roof,
we all end up the same somewhere deep in the dark.

2.
The absence of light.
The absence of breath.
The absence of life.
Praise God almighty, free at last.

Without purposeful intention

Time came to tell me creation will bring its own reward.
The truth wraps me in velvet comfort.
Redundant prayers riddle my consciousness.
Breathe in. Breathe out. Images glisten,
but attenuate to nothing before I divine their meaning.

Banana leaves wrap the ground in pleasure at the rain.
The screech of birds reminds me that this moist jungle
is my only home. Even so my rhythm is faked and insincere.
Or am I wrong? Could this landscape lie,
smiling through its jungle teeth?

A blue feather falls before my face and so I know—
it was serendipity that brought me here, not my birthright.
Beneath the brilliant leaves, years of matter lie,
caked and firm. Until I saw these flowers,
I never knew the meaning of the word red.

Now memory of red grows like weeds
between every thought. I learn to breathe,
and breathing learns my life.
It's a vertical exposure
between here and the void.

Green is a fine way

A mockingbird sings through the humid evening.
The smell of oleander dizzies the dancers into silence.
There is a magic door in a leaf-crept wall, green with portent.

Only the gravest ill can justify such anguish.
The way to the other side is through the ancient door.
Green is a fine way to end one's days.

The peacock angel

Praise Her in five songs,
a vision of the future written on your tongue.
When you look into the mirror to read it,
you lean in close, learn it is written backward.
The tongue and its secrets.
The spurt of the mother
a creamy desecration of the darkness,
a milky way leading through chaos.
I follow you, a mirror held in my hand.
Behind me, you lead.
In front of me, only my own face.

The darkness.
Devils at the door.
Debris twisting in the wind.
The dust outside.
Darkness subsides,
the morning sun reflected in a broken mirror,
the words vaporous signs.
Out of the devastation the new growth,
green as a jungle.

Old ones hidden in the dirt.
A low voice singing.
Greenness a blanket.
The darkness a promise from the night.

ABOUT THE AUTHOR

DONNA J. SNYDER publishes work in literary journals and anthologies throughout the United States and on-line, and has presented readings in Sitka, Alaska, Boston, New York City, Denver, and throughout New Mexico and Texas. Her book reviews appear in *Red Fez*, the *El Paso Times*, and other venues. She is a contributing editor to *Return to Mago*, an international webzine which since 2012 has featured a continuing series of her poems based on the divine feminine principle and the role of women in world culture.

In 2009, El Rancho Press printed a single copy of *Dea Tacita*, as yet disseminated only in public performances. Virgogray Press released her chapbook, *I Am South*, in 2010. In 2015, NeoPoiesis Press will publish her book *Three Sides of the Same Moon*. She is working on a poetry collection for Slough Press.

Snyder's work as an activist lawyer advocating on behalf of indigenous people, immigrant workers, and people with disabilities has garnered multiple prizes and recognitions. She founded the Tumblewords Project in 1995, and continues to coordinate its free weekly workshops and other events.

Publication Credits

These poems have appeared in or are forthcoming from the following publications.

"Daddy? Are you there?" *Dea Tacita*
"I clutch my arms about myself and croon," *Dea Tacita*
"More beautiful with sangria," *Dea Tacita*
"Feather of death," *belindasubraman.com*
"Cinnamon tea," *Chrysalis*
"Dead hands," *Chrysalis, Unlikely Stories 2.0,* and *Boboland Cronicas*
"To Titian's Ariadne," *Return to Mago*
"The truth of Vikings," *The Montucky Review* and *Return to Mago*
"Fierce and fiery to light the long dark," *Newspaper Tree*
"The cruelest month," *Con Tinta NaPoMo 2014*
"Under the fecund moon," *VEXT Magazine*
"Like an angel falling," *VEXT Magazine*

These poems will appear in *Three Sides of the Same Moon*, to be published by NeoPoiesis Press in 2015.

"Where a crone sits alone"
"Silent frogs fiddle"
"Minnow slip of finger"
"Prepare to ululate"
"The truth of Vikings"
"The Sunday news"

To the editors of each of these publications, grateful acknowledgement is made.